Senses in My World
Tasting

by Martha E. H. Rustad

Bullfrog Books

Ideas for Parents and Teachers

Bullfrog Books let children practice reading informational text at the earliest reading levels. Repetition, familiar words, and photo labels support early readers.

Before Reading

- Ask the child to think about senses. Ask: How do you taste?

- Look at the picture glossary together. Read and discuss the words.

Read the Book

- "Walk" through the book and look at the photos. Let the child ask questions. Point out the photo labels.

- Read the book to the child, or have him or her read independently.

After Reading

- Prompt the child to think more. Ask: What type of foods do you taste? How does tasting help you learn about the foods?

Bullfrog Books are published by Jump!
5357 Penn Avenue South
Minneapolis, MN 55419
www.jumplibrary.com

Library of Congress Cataloging-in-Publication Data

Rustad, Martha E. H. (Martha Elizabeth Hillman), 1975- author.
 Tasting / by Martha E.H. Rustad.
   pages cm. — (Senses in my world)
 (Bullfrog books)
 Summary: "This photo-illustrated book for young readers describes how tasting works and the different types of tastes in our food" — Provided by publisher.
 Audience: Ages 5-8.
 Audience: K to grade 3.
 Includes bibliographical references and index.
 ISBN 978-1-62031-118-9 (hardcover) —
 ISBN 978-1-62496-185-4 (ebook) —
 ISBN 978-1-62031-152-3 (paperback)
 1. Tongue — Juvenile literature. 2. Taste buds — Juvenile literature. 3. Taste — Juvenile literature. I. Title.
 QP456.R87 2015
 612.8'7—dc23

                                2013051292

Series Editor: Rebecca Glaser
Series Designer: Ellen Huber
Book Designer: Anna Peterson
Photo Researcher: Kurtis Kinneman

Photo Credits: Getty Images/Andrew Olney, 12; Getty Images/fstop images, 15 (inset); Getty Images/Jose Luis Pelaez Inc, 8–9; iStock/3bugsmom, 10–11; iStock/jcarillet, 14–15, 23mr; iStock/monkeybusinessimages, 20–21; iStock/NatalyaAksenova, 13; iStock/Photolyric, 6–7, 23bl; Shutterstock/Anna Kucherova, 3; Shutterstock/CLIPAREA l Custom media, 6 (inset), 23ml; Shutterstock/Dasha Petrenko, 18–19; Shutterstock/Galushko Sergey, 8 (inset), 23br; Shutterstock/Jag_cz, 23tr; Shutterstock/KIM NGUYEN, 24; Shutterstock/Maks Narodenko, 18 (inset); Shutterstock/Monkey Business Images, 17; Shutterstock/Phaitoon Sutunyawatchai, 1; Shutterstock/Serhiy Kobyakov, 4, 5; Shutterstock/snapgalleria, 22; Shutterstock/Valentyn Volkov, 16, 23tl; Shutterstock/VaLiza, cover

Printed in the United States of America at Corporate Graphics, in North Mankato, Minnesota.
6-2014
10 9 8 7 6 5 4 3 2 1

Table of Contents

How Do We Taste?

Taste is one of our senses. How does it work?

You put food on your tongue.

The little bumps are taste buds.

They send signals.

The brain understands the signals as tastes.

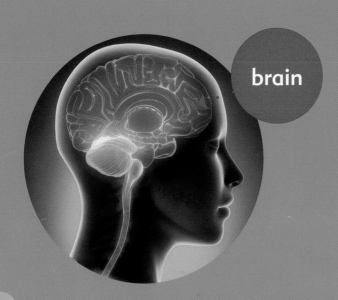

brain

taste
buds

How do foods taste?

Matt eats a cookie.

Yum!

It is sweet.

Mom drinks sour milk.

Yuck!

She knows it is bad.

She throws it away.

Bee eats a chip.

salt

It is salty.

Tim dips a chip in salsa.

It is too spicy.

Dad sips black coffee.

coffee

It has a bitter taste.

But he likes it.

Two girls try a green apple.

It has a sour taste.

Amy likes it.

Jen does not.

What tastes do you like?

Parts of the Mouth

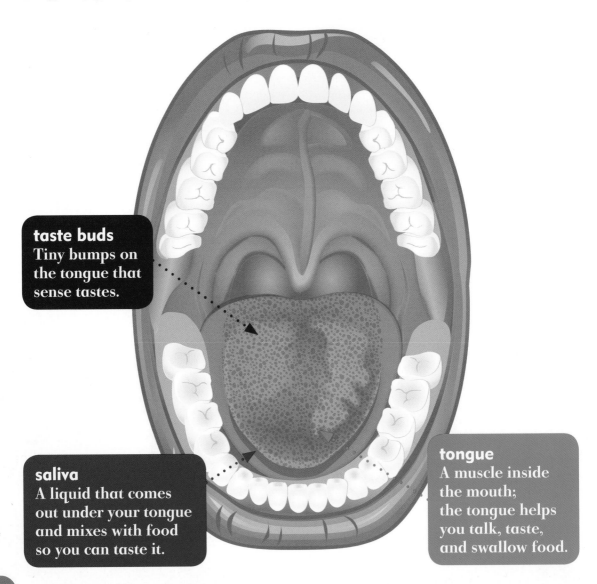

taste buds
Tiny bumps on the tongue that sense tastes.

saliva
A liquid that comes out under your tongue and mixes with food so you can taste it.

tongue
A muscle inside the mouth; the tongue helps you talk, taste, and swallow food.

Picture Glossary

bitter
Tasting harsh and sharp, such as coffee.

sour
Tasting acidic and sharp, such as a lemon.

brain
A body part in your head that helps you think and understand.

spicy
Flavored with lots of spices, such as salsa or chili.

sense
A way of knowing about things around you; you have five senses.

sweet
Tasting like sugar or honey, such as candy or cookies.

Index

To Learn More

Learning more is as easy as 1, 2, 3.

1) Go to www.factsurfer.com

2) Enter "tasting" into the search box.

3) Click the "Surf" button to see a list of websites.

With factsurfer.com, finding more information is just a click away.